Bilingual Edition

Clean and Healthy / Limpieza y salud

Edición Bilingüe

Brushing My Teeth
¡A lavarse los dientes!

Elizabeth Vogel
Traducción al español:
Tomás González

The Rosen Publishing Group's
PowerKids Press™ & **Editorial Buenas Letras**™
New York

1

Published in 2001, 2003 by The Rosen Publishing Group, Inc.
29 East 21st Street, New York, NY 10010

First Bilingual Edition 2003
First English Edition 2001

Book Design: Felicity Erwin
Layout: Dean Galiano

Photographs by Cindy Reiman

Vogel, Elizabeth.
　　Brushing my teeth = ¡A lavarse los dientes! / by Elizabeth Vogel ; traducción al español Tomás González.
　　　　p. cm.— (PowerKids Readers, Clean and healthy all day long = Limpieza y salud todo el día)
　　Includes index.
　　Summary: A girl describes how she brushes her teeth and how the process cleans off plaque and helps to keep her mouth safe from unhealthy germs.
　　ISBN 0-8239-6621-6 (lib. bdg. : alk. paper)
　　1. Teeth—Care and hygiene—Juvenile literature. 2. Teeth—Juvenile literature. [1.Teeth—Care and hygiene. 2. Spanish language materials—Bilingual] I. Title. II. Series.
　　617.6'01—dc21

Manufactured in the United States of America.

2

Contents

Contenido

I brush my teeth every morning and every night. I make sure to keep my teeth very clean.

———

Me lavo los dientes cada mañana y cada noche. Me gusta mantener los dientes muy limpios.

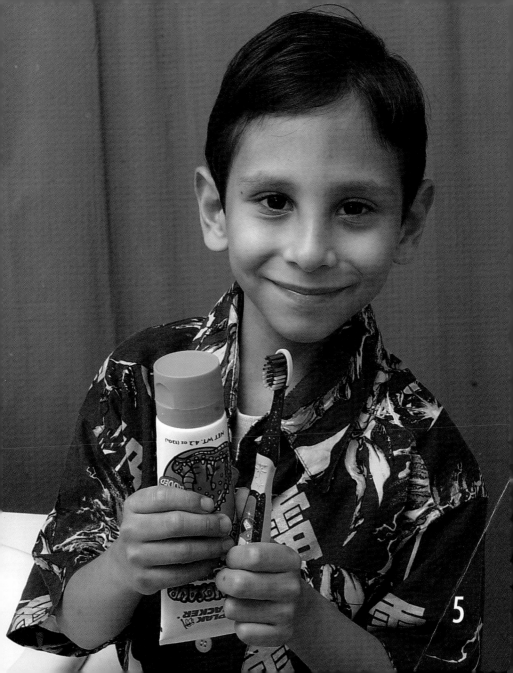

I turn on the water at the sink to wet my toothbrush.

Abro la llave del lavabo para mojar el cepillo.

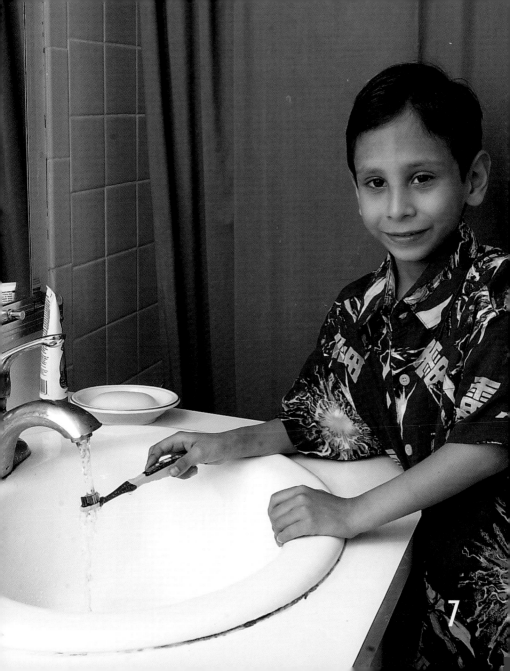

My dad helps me squeeze the toothpaste onto my toothbrush. The toothpaste tastes like bubble gum.

Mi papá me ayuda a ponerle crema dental al cepillo. La crema dental sabe como goma de mascar.

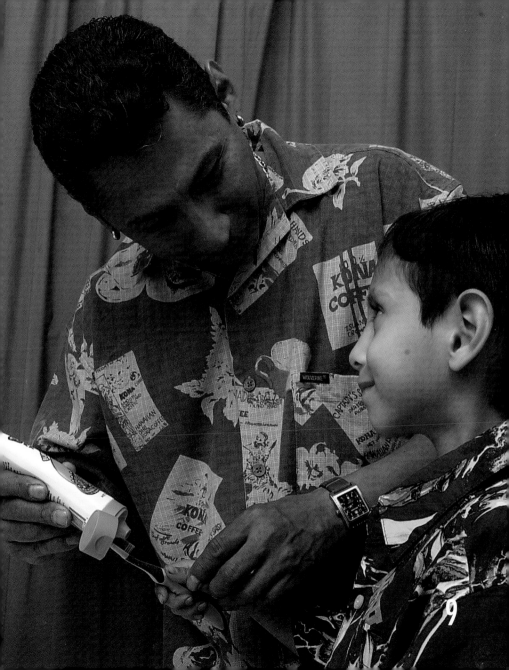

My dad tells me that brushing helps keep my whole mouth safe from unhealthy germs.

———

Mi papá dice que al cepillarme los dientes no dejo que vivan en mi boca gérmenes dañinos.

11

I brush my teeth in small, gentle circles. I brush one or two teeth at a time. Brush! Brush!

Me cepillo en pequeños círculos, con mucha suavidad. Cepillo uno o dos dientes a la vez.

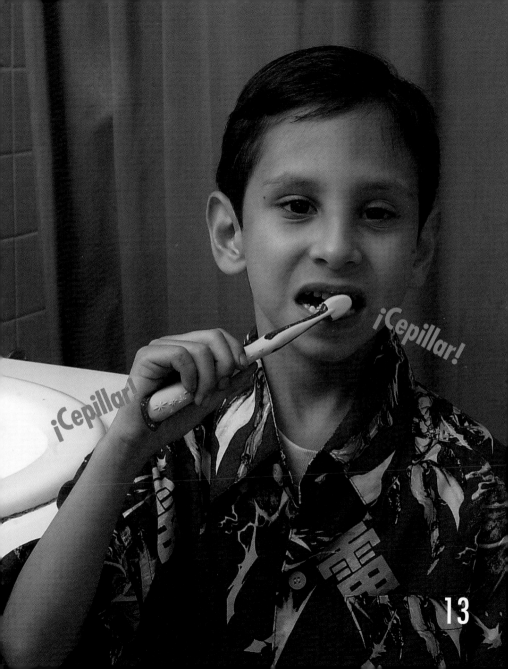

¡Cepillar!

¡Cepillar!

13

My dad tells me we brush our teeth to clean off plaque. Plaque is a coating that covers teeth. Plaque can cause cavities.

———

Mi papá dice que nos cepillamos para mantener los dientes sin placa dental. La placa es una sustancia que cubre los dientes y causa caries.

14

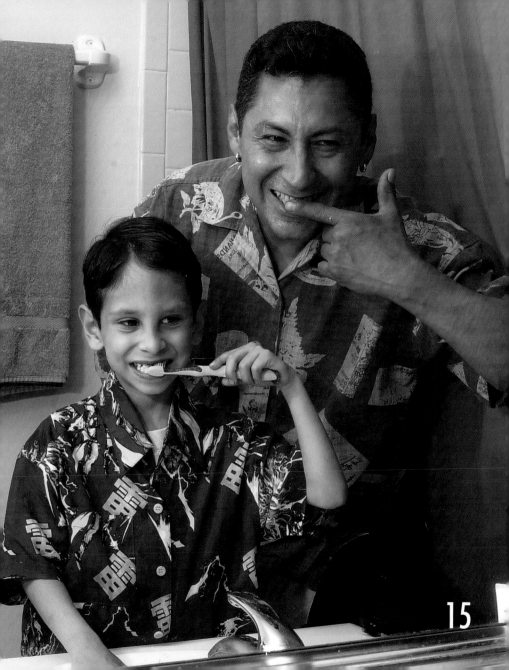

I remember to brush my tongue, too. Germs can also live on your tongue.

———————

No me olvido de cepillarme la lengua. Los gérmenes también pueden vivir en la lengua.

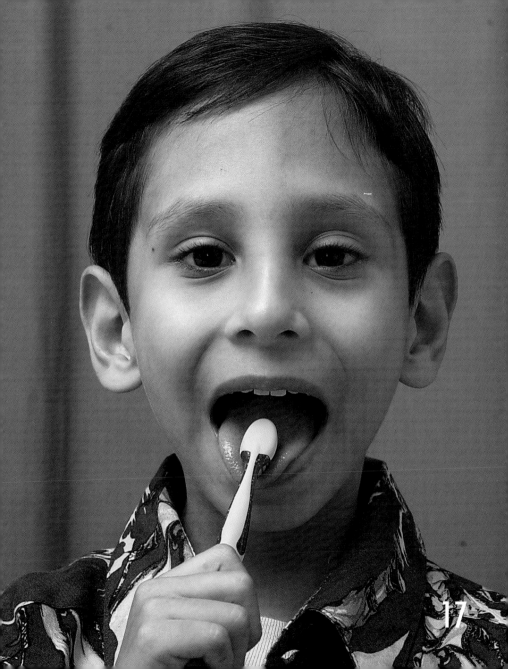

I fill my cup with water and get ready to rinse my mouth.

———————

Lleno de agua mi vaso, para enjuagarme la boca.

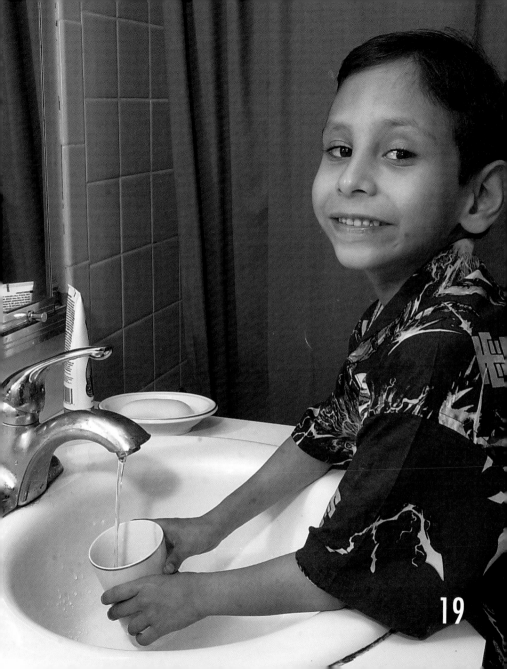

After I am done brushing
I like to smile and look at
my clean and healthy
teeth!

Cuando termino de
cepillarme me gusta
sonreír. ¡Mis dientes se
ven limpios y sanos!

Words to Know
Palabras que debes saber

CUP /
VASO

SINK /
LAVABO

TEETH /
DIENTES

TONGUE /
LENGUA

TOOTHBRUSH /
CEPILLO DE DIENTES

TOOTHPASTE /
CREMA DENTAL

Here are more books to read about brushing your teeth / Otros libros que puedes leer sobre el cepillado de los dientes:

In English / En inglés:
Brushing Well
por Helen Frost
Pebble Books

Bilingual Editions / Ediciones bilingües:
Those Icky Sticky Smelly Cavity-Causing but...
Invisible Germs / Esos sucios pegajosos olorosos
causantes de caries... pero invisibles gérmenes
Bilingual Children's Health Series
por Judith Anne Rice
Redleaf Press, 1997

Due to the changing nature of Internet links, PowerKids Press has developed an online list of Web sites related to the subject of this book. This site is updated regularly. Please use this link to access the list:

http://www.buenasletraslinks.com/chl/bmt

Index

Índice

Words in English: 147   Palabras en español: 139

Note to Parents, Teachers, and Librarians

PowerKids Readers en Español are specially designed to get emergent and beginning hispanic readers excited about learning to read. Simple stories and concepts are paired with photographs of real kids in real-life situations. Sentences are short and simple, employing a basic vocabulary of sight words, as well as new words that describe familiar things and places. With their engaging stories and vivid photo-illustrations, PowerKids en Español gives children the opportunity to develop a love of reading and learning that they will carry with them throughout their lives.